Stations of the Nativity

Illustrations by Patrick Kelley

with text by Lawrence Boadt, C.S.P.

Paulist Press
New York/Mahwah, N.J.

Artist's dedication
To the B.V.M., all my love.
Totus tuus, too.
P.K.

Author's dedication
To all the employees of Paulist Press
who make such beautiful books as this happen.
L.B.

Caseside and interior design by Lynn Else

Text Copyright © 2002 by Paulist Press Inc.
Illustrations Copyright © 2002 by Patrick Kelley

Original biblical translation by Lawrence Boadt, C.S.P.

Library of Congress Cataloging-in-Publication

Boadt Lawrence.
Stations of the Nativity / by Lawrence Boadt.
p. cm.
Summary: Meditations on fourteen well-known incidents surrounding the birth of Jesus.
ISBN 0-8091-6699-2 (alk. paper)
1. Jesus Christ—Nativity—Prayer-books and devotions—English. 2. Christian children—Prayer-books and devotions—English. [1. Jesus Christ—Nativity. 2. Prayer-books and devotions.] I. Title.

BT315.3 .B63 2002
232.92—dc21
2001056013

Published by Paulist Press
997 Macarthur Boulevard
Mahwah, New Jersey 07430

www.paulistpress.com

Printed and bound in Mexico

Stations of the Nativity

How to Use

Here is a brand new way to celebrate Advent and the Christmas season. As in the Lenten Stations, fourteen scenes from Jesus' life are used as opportunities for prayer. The familiar scenes here are those surrounding Christ's birth. For each, there is a New Testament verse, a short meditation, a lesson, a prayer, and a psalm verse. All of these bring out the meaning of the scene for our own lives today.

The Stations of the Nativity can be prayed alone or with others. They can be used at home, school, or wherever small groups gather to share their faith. The Stations can replace a worn-out Advent wreath or be used along with it to give new life to an old tradition.

While the readings are seasonal, how and when you pray the Stations is up to you. Pray through the entire book in one sitting. Pray a page a day for the two weeks before Christmas. Pray the Stations daily from Christmas Eve through Epiphany. Or pray them throughout the year as a reminder of Christ's incarnation among us.

First Station
The Annunciation

Reading

And the angel said to her, "Fear not, Mary, for you have found favor with God. You will bear a son and call his name Jesus, and he will be great"…And Mary said, "Behold the handmaid of the Lord: let it be done to me according to your word." (Luke 1:30–31, 38)

Meditation

We do not know Mary before this moment, but we quickly discover her loving spirit. She has a deep sense of God's presence and a willingness to let God lead her wherever he wants. Despite her fears, she gives a truly humble and faithful "yes" to whatever God asks.

Lesson

Mary is the first person to say the powerful words that Jesus will later teach all his disciples to pray: "Thy will be done." (Matt 6:10)

Prayer

Lord God, you who do miracles in the souls of those who love you, help each of us to cooperate with your grace in our lives and to give our will to you without reserve. Amen.

Psalm Verse

Whoever has clean hands and a pure heart and does not act with vanity or swear falsely shall receive blessing from the Lord and righteousness from the God of salvation. (Ps 24:4–5)

Second Station
The Visitation

Reading

When Elizabeth heard Mary's greeting, the baby leapt in her womb, and Elizabeth was filled with the Holy Spirit and spoke with a loud voice, saying, "Blessed are you among women, and blessed is the fruit of your womb." (Luke 1:41–42)

Meditation

The grace of the Holy Spirit helped Elizabeth "see" that Mary was specially blessed by God with a child who would do wonderful things for all people. Elizabeth was also able to understand that Mary had accepted this gift with love and faithfulness. We, too, can pay attention to the Spirit, which will help us know what is right and help us feel the joy and peace of always choosing God's will.

Lesson

This beautiful passage contains the words we say when we pray the *Hail Mary*. The *Hail Mary* reminds us of God's constant guidance, the joy of obeying him, and the example of Mary and Elizabeth.

Prayer

O God, teach me the joy and happiness of doing your will always, and seeing your love and goodness in everyone whom I greet this day. Amen.

Psalm Verse

Our soul waits for the Lord who is our help and our shield. Our hearts will rejoice in him because we have trusted in his holy name. (Ps 33:20–21)

Third Station
The Magnificat, the Song of Mary

Reading

"My soul glorifies the Lord and my spirit rejoices in God my savior ... for he that is mighty has done great things for me…His mercy is on those who fear him in every generation…He fills the hungry with good things…and he helps his servant Israel." (Luke 1:46–47, 49–50, 53–54)

Meditation

Mary sings one of the most famous songs in the Bible. She thanks God for the great blessing he has brought her, but she does not dwell on her own importance. She quickly goes on to remember all the times God has helped Israel. She moves past her own good fortune to praise God for saving the poor, the hungry, and the humble.

Lesson

The best and easiest prayer is to praise God and to thank him for the many small ways in which he blesses us and helps us in ordinary things.

Prayer

Through the help of Mary, our Mother, may God make the sick well, the troubled calm, and the wounded healed. Amen.

Psalm Verse

Hannah prayed and said, "My heart rejoices in the Lord; my horn is exalted in the Lord; my mouth boasts over my enemies, because I rejoice in your salvation. There is none holy as the Lord; there is none beside you; there is no rock like our God." (1 Sam 2:1–2)

Fourth Station

The Birth of John the Baptist

Reading

Elizabeth's time came for delivery, and she gave birth to a son, and her neighbors and relatives …rejoiced with her….They made signs to [the child's] father how he would name him,…and he wrote, "His name is John."
(Luke 1:57–58, 62, 63)

Meditation

St. Luke weaves the birth of John the Baptist into the story of how Jesus was born, because they are closely related in God's plan. The name "John" means "God gives favor" or "God has mercy." John will go before Jesus to announce his coming as the day of God's favor, mercy, and salvation for the whole world. John will call on everyone who hears him to repent and to prepare for the Lord.

Lesson

John is a prophet who makes known the good news that the Messiah and Savior has come. We need to open our eyes and recognize that truth in our own lives.

Prayer

Father, you sent John the Baptist before your Son to warn us to give up our sins and to seek your forgiveness. May we recognize Jesus when he comes into our lives and welcome his love into our hearts. Amen.

Psalm Verse

Show me your ways, O Lord, and teach me your paths. Lead me in your truth and teach me, for you are the God of my salvation. I wait for you all the day long.
(Ps 25:4–5)

Fifth Station
The Prophecy of Zechariah

Reading

Zechariah was filled with the Holy Spirit and prophesied, saying, "Blessed be the Lord God of Israel, for he has visited and redeemed his people…that we might serve him without fear, holy and righteous in his sight all the days of our life." (Luke 1:67–68, 74–75)

Meditation

Zechariah, John's father, is given the gift to foresee that his child will become the greatest prophet of all time. John will prepare the way for Jesus. In Jesus, God remembers his covenant with his servant Israel, offers forgiveness of sins, and brings peace and light to all peoples of the world.

Lesson

Prophets remind us that God promises forgiveness and healing despite our bad deeds and sins. We need to hear this message often so we do not forget to turn back to God every time we fail.

Prayer

O God, who sent John the Baptist to remind us of your eternal mercy, grant that we turn from our sins and treat one another with justice, love, and respect always. Amen.

Psalm Verse

I will sing the mercies of the Lord forever; I will make known your faithfulness to all generations….And the heavens shall praise your wonders, O Lord; your faithfulness in the assembly of the saints. (Ps 89:1, 5)

Sixth Station

Joseph's Dream

Reading

Behold, the angel of the Lord appeared to Joseph in a dream, saying, "Joseph, you son of David, fear not to take to yourself Mary your wife…She shall bring forth a son and you will call his name Jesus, for he will save his people from their sins." (Matt 1:20, 21)

Meditation

Joseph loved Mary, his bride-to-be, but what of the child she was clearly carrying? He decided to send Mary away. Then Joseph was visited by an angel and told of the child's divine origin. Should Joseph now do what society expected, or make the more difficult choice and listen to the word of God?

Lesson

Learn to look to God when things seem bad, and to pray at once for God's help in knowing how to do what is right.

Prayer

God our Father, help us to imitate the faith and trust of Joseph, the earthly guardian of your divine Son Jesus, and to seek your help in all our troubles. Amen.

Psalm Verse

In you, O Lord, I put my trust; never let me be left confused; rescue me in your justice and let me escape. Incline your ear to me and save me. (Ps 71:1–2)

Seventh Station

Joseph Takes Mary into His Home

Reading

Then Joseph awakened from sleep and did as the angel of the Lord had commanded him and received Mary as his wife. And she…brought forth her firstborn son, and [Joseph] called his name Jesus. (Matt 1:24–25)

Meditation

The angel told Joseph to name the child *Jesus*. In Hebrew this means "God saves" his people. The angel also gave the child a second name, *Emmanuel.* This means "God is with us." When Joseph woke, he received the blessing of this name right away. His decision was difficult, but he acted with faith and obeyed God's word. By bringing Mary and her baby into his home, Joseph truly had God with him.

Lesson

When we keep God's commandments and express our love to him in prayer, we can be sure that God dwells within us, and that he aids us in everything we do.

Prayer

O Loving Father, you sent your Son Jesus to live with us on earth that we might live with him forever in heaven. Grant that we may stay close to him all the days of our lives. Amen.

Psalm Verse

How lovely is your dwelling place, O Lord of Hosts. My soul longs and hungers for the courtyards of the Lord. (Ps 84:1–2)

Eighth Station
The Journey to Bethlehem

Reading

And Joseph went up from Galilee from the town of Nazareth into Judea, to the city of David which is called Bethlehem, with his engaged wife Mary, who was near to giving birth, in order to pay the tax there. (Luke 2:4–5)

Meditation

Until now, the events preparing for the birth of Jesus seem guided by God's hand, often through miracles and dreams. But now a long difficult trip had to be made, commanded by Rome. Even when Joseph and Mary arrived in Bethlehem, their problems were not over; there was no room at the inn. If they were following God's word, why wasn't life easier?

Lesson

In our everyday life, we often have to accept pain or difficulties in order to gain something better. Gaining the ultimate — the kingdom of heaven — may ask of us even more.

Prayer

O Lord, be with us in every pain and difficulty, and give us the courage to put up with hardships in our lives. Let us serve you as faithfully as did Mary and Joseph. Amen.

Psalm Verse

The Lord will deliver them in the time of trouble. The Lord will protect them and keep them alive and they shall be blessed upon the earth. (Ps 41:1–2)

Ninth Station
The Birth of Jesus

Reading

And so it was, that while they were there, her days were completed so that she was to give birth. And she brought forth her first-born son and wrapped him in swaddling clothes, and laid him in a manger, because there was no room for them in the inn. (Luke 2:6–7)

Meditation

In a barn, there among God's beloved animals, Jesus was born. He came into the world as small and helpless as any human being ever did. This way he could be a friend and savior for every kind of person: rich or poor, young or old, important or unimportant.

Lesson

By coming as the least of creatures, Jesus shows that God will work great things for all people and also that all people should be treated equally with love and respect, just as Jesus always treated them.

Prayer

O God of all love and mercy, look upon us with kindness when we are most in need and the least important in the eyes of others. Help us also to imitate the love and kindness Jesus had for all people. Amen.

Psalm Verse

Have mercy upon me, O Lord, for I am weak; O Lord, heal me, for my bones are wounded. My soul also is troubled….Return, Lord, deliver my soul for your mercy's sake. (Ps 6:2–4)

Tenth Station

The Announcement of the Angels

Reading

And there were shepherds in the same area watching their flocks by night, and behold the angel of the Lord appeared to them...and said, "Fear not, I bring you good news of great joy to all peoples, for unto you is born this day in the city of David a savior, who is Christ the Lord." (Luke 2:8–11)

Meditation

The angels said "Fear not." These words are repeated often in the Bible. The ways of God are great and mysterious and can sometimes be frightening. But they are also filled with love for each of his creatures, for *all* of his creatures. Here were words of the greatest love, that a savior had come for all peoples.

Lesson

Let me listen to the word of God without fear, but rather with quiet rejoicing in my heart, knowing that Jesus came for me.

Prayer

O Lord our God, who made all things out of love, help me to give you thanks and praise always for your goodness and to see your loving hand in my life. Amen.

Psalm Verse

Bless the Lord, O my soul…How many are your works, O Lord; and in wisdom you have made them all; the earth is full of your creatures. (Ps 104:1, 24)

Eleventh Station
The Shepherds Share the Good News

Reading

The shepherds said to one another, "Let us go then to Bethlehem and see this event which the Lord has made known to us." So they went in haste and found Mary and Joseph, and the baby lying in the manger. When they had seen him, they spread the word concerning what had been told them about this child. (Luke 2:15–17)

Meditation

If someone became king today, who would be told first? Other kings, presidents, the rich, and the powerful? Yet when Jesus, King of Kings, was born, the news was told first to the lowly. Though simple people, the shepherds recognized God's work hidden in the stable. Amazed by what they saw, the shepherds then told everyone they knew and praised God aloud for his goodness.

Lesson

Listen to those who remain simple and humble in spirit, as God is in their lives.

Prayer

O Lord, open my ears to everyone who speaks your name, and loosen my tongue at every chance to praise you. Amen.

Psalm Verse

Sing joyfully to the Lord, you righteous; it is fitting for the upright to praise him…For the word of the Lord is right and true; he is faithful in all he does. (Ps 33:1, 4)

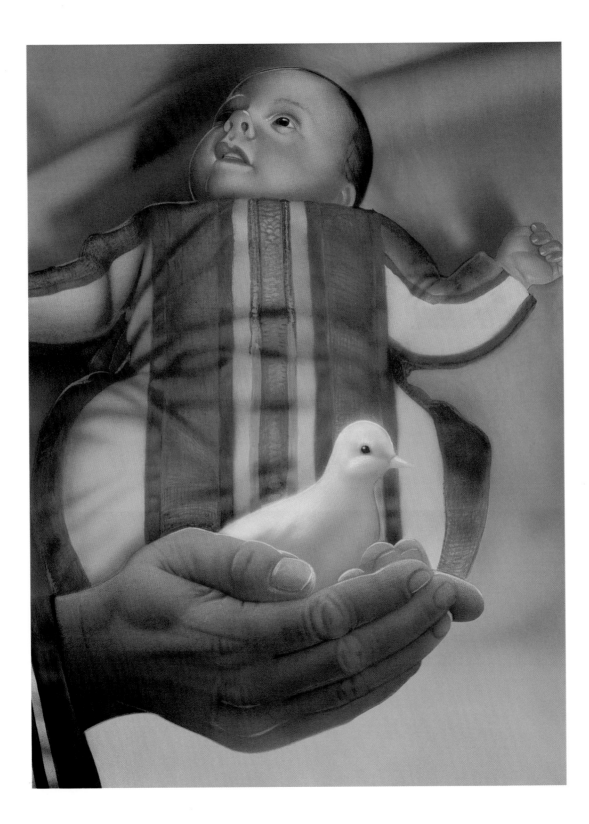

Twelfth Station
The Presentation of Jesus in the Temple

Reading

They took him up to Jerusalem to present him to the Lord…in accordance with the commandment in the Law of the Lord. (Luke 2:22, 24)

Meditation

It is an important commandment in the Jewish faith that the firstborn is brought to the temple to be offered to God for blessing. The first child of a family represents the special love God had for the whole Jewish people when he saved them from slavery in Egypt and made them his chosen people.

Lesson

The ceremony of offering a child to God reminds us that each of us is chosen by God. We, too, become God's special people by the sacrament of baptism.

Prayer

Lord God, you care for us with the love of both a father and a mother. Keep us close to you as part of your family. Help each of us to act as a true child of God in everything that we do. Amen.

Psalm Verse

You who dwell in the shadow of the Almighty, say to the Lord, "My refuge and my fortress, my God in whom I trust…With his feathers he will cover you; under his wings you shall take refuge." (Ps 91:1, 2, 4)

Thirteenth Station
The Blessing of Simeon

Reading

Simeon took the boy into his arms and blessed God, saying: "Now Lord, you may let your servant die in peace. For according to your word, my eyes have seen your salvation, which you prepared in the sight of all peoples, a light of revelation for the pagans and the glory of your people Israel." (Luke 2:28–32)

Meditation

When Mary and Joseph brought Jesus to the temple, they met two holy prophets, Simeon and Anna. Simeon rejoiced that his life was now complete because he saw in the child the savior of the whole world. Anna, whose words followed, praised God as well, then told everyone that the redeemer had been sent.

Lesson

Who were the first to recognize Jesus? First a minor priest, Zechariah, and his wife, Elizabeth; then shepherds; then two elderly people, prophets. Over and over, it is through ordinary people that God's message is heard and shared.

Prayer

Oh God of all love, help me to see your face in the faces of my friends and enemies alike, and to treat every human being as a gift from you, deserving my love. Amen.

Psalm Verse

Your faithfulness and your salvation I have made known [O Lord], I have not kept secret your kindness and your truth in the whole community. Do not keep your mercy from me, but may your kindness and your truth always protect me. (Ps 39:11–12)

Reading

When Jesus was born in Bethlehem of Judea...wise men came from the East to Jerusalem, saying, "Where is the new-born king of the Jews? We have seen his star at its rising and have come to pay him honor." (Matt 2: 1–2)

Meditation

The story of the wise men from the East showed that even foreigners recognized that salvation had come. They traveled into the unknown, both the unknown land of Israel and the unknown land of a world touched by God.

Lesson

In a way, we are all foreigners. We come from a world of anger and hatred, and look for the kingdom of God—a world of justice, peace, and

love. Like the wise men, we need to humble ourselves to do what God wants, even to traveling into the unknown to find him.

Prayer

O great God, bless your children everywhere, and help all people to love one another and live at peace with one another. Amen.

Psalm Verse

All kings shall bow down before him, all nations shall serve him; for he shall rescue the poor man when he cries out, and the humble person when he has no one to help him. (Ps 72:11–12)

Note on Praying with
Stations of the Nativity

For the young and the old and everyone in between, the Stations of the Nativity are a wonderful way to observe Advent and Christmas. Let them find their place beside the Advent wreath and other traditional practices of the season.

The Stations of the Nativity are also a unique way to meditate on the glory of the Incarnation the whole year long. Jesus enters our lives every day. The Stations of the Nativity give us a focus through which to think about how he appears to us and what our response to him should be.

※ ※ ※

Whether praying the Stations of the Nativity alone or in a group, you may prefer to use the extended Scripture passage. Here are the citations:

First Station, The Annunciation—Luke 1:26–38

Second Station, The Visitation—Luke 1:39–45

Third Station, The Song of Mary *(Magnificat)*—Luke 1:46–55

Fourth Station, The Birth of John the Baptist—Luke 1:57–66

Fifth Station, The Prophecy of Zechariah—Luke 1:67–79

Sixth Station, Joseph's Dream—Matthew 1:18–23

Seventh Station, Joseph Takes Mary into His Home—Matthew 1:24–25

Eighth Station, The Journey to Bethlehem—Luke 2:1–5

Ninth Station, The Birth of Jesus—Luke 2:6–7

Tenth Station, The Announcement of the Angels—Luke 2:8–14

Eleventh Station, The Shepherds Share the Good News—Luke 2:15–20

Twelfth Station, The Presentation of Jesus in the Temple—Luke 2:22–24

Thirteenth Station, The Blessing of Simeon—Luke 25–38

Fourteenth Station, The Wise Men Come from the East—Matthew 2:1–12